For Vicky

ABOUT THE BOOK:

Here is a collection of amazing-but-true stories about some of
football's most colorful players, unusual (and often funny) situations,
and breath-taking plays. There is the player who ran the wrong
way with the ball and scored for the wrong team, the rookie who
scored a touchdown on his very first play in a pro game, the teams
that played a championship game during a terrible blizzard, and
the quarterback who caught his own pass. Johnny Unitas, Gale
Sayers, Norm Van Brocklin, and Garo Yepremian are among the
famous stars included in the book.

ABOUT THE AUTHOR:

A former teacher, Mel Cebulash now works as an editor for
Scholastic Book Services, where he specializes in easy-to-read
materials. He is the author of *Baseball Players Do Amazing Things* as
well as several books distributed by the Scholastic organization. Mr.
Cebulash lives in New York City.

Cover picture: Garo Yepremian makes his one and only pass, January 14, 1973.

BOOK CLUB EDITION

Football Players Do Amazing Things

by Mel Cebulash

Illustrated with photographs

Step-Up Books   **Random House**

New York

Photograph credits: United Press International, end papers, 8, 15, 17, 23, 25, 28, 29, 33, 34, 36, 38, 42, 44, 45, 48, 50, 51, 55, 64; Wide World Photos, 12, 13, 21, 27, 35, 40, 54, 60, 62, 67.
Cover: Photo by Al Satterwhite (Camera 5)

Library of Congress Cataloging in Publication Data   Cebulash, Mel.   Football players do amazing things.   (Step-up books)   1. Football—History—Juvenile literature. [1. Football—History]   I. Title.   GV954.C42   796.33'2   73-3686   ISBN: 0-394-82677-9   ISBN: 0-394-92677-3 (library edition)

Manufactured in the United States of America

A B C D E   6 7 8 9 0

CONTENTS

Jim Marshall just ran 60 yards. Why does he look so sad?

A 60-Yard Run

October 25, 1964. The Minnesota Vikings were playing the San Francisco Forty-Niners in San Francisco.

The opening kickoff went to Minnesota. The Vikings fumbled, and San Francisco got the ball. The Forty-Niners ran a few plays. Then they scored a touchdown. The score was San Francisco 7, Minnesota 0.

Again Minnesota fumbled the kickoff. This time the Forty-Niners did not score. But when they punted to Minnesota, the Vikings fumbled again. Now the Minnesota team had fumbled three times in a row.

While the Vikings were fumbling the ball, the Forty-Niners were making bad passes. Twice, Forty-Niner end-zone passes fell into Viking hands. The fans were watching a game of mistakes.

In spite of the mistakes, both teams scored. At the end of the first half, the Forty-Niners led, 17–10.

The Vikings played a little better in the second half. And early in the fourth quarter, they went ahead, 20–17. Minutes later a Forty-Niner fumble gave them another touchdown and a 27–17 lead.

After the kickoff, the Forty-Niners started to move again. And then the most amazing play of the day began.

First, Forty-Niner running back Billy Kilmer caught a pass. But the Vikings went after him, and he lost the ball. Viking end Jim Marshall picked it up and raced for the goal line.

As he ran the 60 yards to the goal, Marshall heard cheering. He crossed into the end zone and tossed the ball into the air. He thought he had scored a touchdown.

But then a Forty-Niner hugged Marshall and thanked him. Marshall wondered why. He looked around.

Suddenly he saw what had happened. He had run 60 yards. But he had run the wrong way! He had not scored a touchdown. He had scored a safety for the other team. He had given the Forty-Niners two points and cut his own team's lead to 27–19.

Jim Marshall picks up a Forty-Niner fumble.

He runs with the ball—the wrong way.   A Forty-Niner thanks him.

Jim Marshall felt sick. His wrong-way run was the most amazing mistake in a game full of mistakes.

"Forget about it," Marshall's coach told him.

For the rest of the game Marshall played hard and well. And his team finally won, 27–22.

Jim Marshall probably never forgot his wrong-way run. But he did not let it stop him. He understood that the best of players make mistakes—even big ones.

Marshall tries to explain his wrong-way run.

An Air Show

The most important player on a football team is the quarterback. In the 1950s the quarterback for the Los Angeles Rams was Bob Waterfield. He was their star player. His fans came to every game hoping to see him score for the Rams. In game after game, he made the fans happy.

But on the sidelines Norm Van Brocklin was not so happy. He was waiting to play. He was the Rams' second-string quarterback. He could play only if Bob Waterfield could not.

At last on September 28, 1951, Norm Van Brocklin got his chance. The Rams were playing a New York team called the Yanks. Bob Waterfield

was hurt. He could
not play. So Van
Brocklin took his place.
Van Brocklin knew he
would have to do some
great playing to make
the fans forget Bob
Waterfield.

Van Brocklin wasted no time.
Making one perfect pass after another,
he moved the Rams down the field. By
the end of the quarter, his passes had
given the Rams a 21–0 lead.

In the second quarter, Van
Brocklin's sharp passing gained many
more yards for the Rams. And when
they got near the goal line, they
pushed across it. By halftime the score
was Rams 34, Yanks 7.

The Yanks tried hard to stop Van Brocklin in the third quarter. But his passes kept on finding their man and gaining yards for the Rams. Near the end of the quarter, his fourth touchdown pass put the Rams ahead by 41–7.

Van Brocklin kept up his air show in the fourth quarter. Every time he passed, the ball landed in the arms of a Ram player.

The Yanks kept trying. At one point Van Brocklin had moved the Rams to the Yanks' 1-yard line. The Yanks dug in. They did not want to let the Rams score another touchdown.

Van Brocklin took a chance. Instead of trying to run for the yard, he got set to pass. He let the ball fly. It sailed

Norm Van Brocklin (11) passes the ball.

into the waiting arms of Crazy Legs
Hirsch. Hirsch was over the goal for
a touchdown. The pass was Van
Brocklin's shortest of the day. But it
was his fifth touchdown throw.

The Yanks finally scored again. But their seven points did not make much difference. The final score was Rams 54, Yanks 14.

Norm Van Brocklin had put on a real air show. He had completed 27 out of 41 passes. And his passes had moved the Rams 554 yards. He had set a new record for yards gained through passing. And that record still stands.

The fans yelled and clapped for Van Brocklin. He had shown them some amazing passing. And just think— Norm Van Brocklin would not have played quarterback if Bob Waterfield had been well!

Last Play of the Day

November 8, 1970. The Detroit Lions were playing the New Orleans Saints. New Orleans had a weak team that year. It had won only one game in seven. The fans were sure the Lions would beat the Saints easily.

As the game went on, the Saints surprised the large crowd. They played hard and well. They were giving the Lions a real fight. In the fourth quarter, the Saints were ahead, 16–14.

With 11 seconds left in the game, the Lions scored a field goal. It put them ahead, 17–16. Everyone thought that the Lions had won the game. The New Orleans fans got ready to leave.

With only 11 seconds left, they did not think the Saints would have time to score.

The Saints returned the kickoff to their own 28-yard line. Then a pass moved the Saints 17 yards. The play went out of bounds. So the clock was stopped with two seconds left in the game.

How could the Saints score in only two seconds? Their coach decided to have Tom Dempsey try for a field goal. No other play would give the Saints much chance to score. A kick by Dempsey was their best bet to win the game.

Tom Dempsey ran onto the field. Tom had already kicked three field goals that day. But this kick would be much harder. This time the ball was going to be placed down on his 37-yard line. His kick would have to go through the goalposts 63 yards away.

No one in professional football had

ever kicked a 63-yard field goal. The record kick was 56 yards. And it had been in the record book for 17 years.

The Saints lined up for the play. The ball was set into place. Then Tom Dempsey started his short run at it.

Dempsey's right foot hit the ball and lifted it. The crowd watched the football rise. Their eyes followed it. To them the kick looked good. They waited.

Then they saw the signal. It *was* good! Tom Dempsey had kicked a 63-yard field goal. He had kicked the longest field goal in professional football history. The game was over. The Saints had won, 19–17.

The other Saints ran over to Tom Dempsey. They lifted him up and carried him off the field. The crowd stood and cheered. They had watched a fine game with an amazing ending.

After the game, Tom Dempsey took off his right shoe. It was a special shoe made just for Tom. It had a thick

leather plate on the front end to give him a surface for kicking the football. Tom Dempsey had been born with only half a right foot and no right hand. But the amazing Tom Dempsey had never let that stop him.

First and Last Pass

Most professional football players are tall men with big shoulders. They play a hard game. So they need to be heavy and strong. But a few players are different. One of them is Garo Yepremian.

Garo never looked a bit like a football player. He was bald, lightweight, and short. He was almost a foot shorter than many of the players on his team. But he was one of the best kickers in football.

Garo learned to kick by playing soccer on Cyprus, an island near Greece. He lived there until he was 22. Then in 1966 he came to the United States. He was still a soccer player.

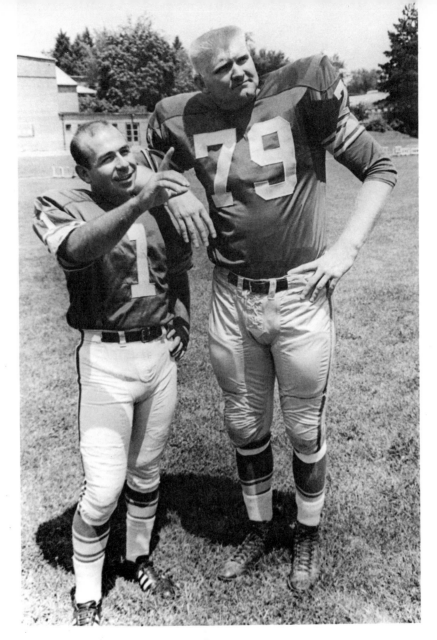

Garo Yepremian and a teammate.

But his brother thought he could use his kicking skills in football. Garo tried out for the Detroit Lions. He made the team.

In 1970 he joined the Miami Dolphins. With them he became a star kicker. And though he was small, he kicked many long field goals.

On January 14, 1973, the Miami Dolphins were playing the Washington Redskins in the Super Bowl.

The Dolphins had not lost a game all year. And by halftime they were leading the Redskins, 14–0.

The third quarter passed without a score by either team. And when the clock showed seven minutes left in the game, the Dolphins still led, 14–0.

Then the Dolphins lined up for a try

at a 43-yard field goal.
If the kick was good, the
Redskins would not have
much hope of winning.

Garo Yepremian ran
onto the field. Miami
fans cheered. They were
sure Garo could kick the
ball 43 yards.

The football came
back. Garo took a few
short steps and kicked it.
The ball hit a Dolphin player and
bounced back to Garo. The little
kicking star picked up the football and
started to run. Then he saw the
Redskins coming at him.

Without thinking, Garo got set to
pass the ball. But he was a kicker.

A kicker is not supposed to do anything but kick. And so Garo had never passed a football before.

He swung his arm forward to pass the ball. But the ball did not go forward. It flew out of his small hand, straight up into the air. It dropped right into the hands of Mike Bass, a Redskin back.

Bass raced down the sidelines. Before

Garo makes his only pass.

the Dolphins could catch him, he scored a touchdown.

It was a funny play. The Redskins on the sidelines laughed. The fans laughed, too.

But the play was not funny to Garo. He wished he had not tried to pass. Why hadn't he just fallen on the ball? He did not look forward to facing his coach and teammates.

Mike Bass catches the ball.

Bass runs for a touchdown.

Now the Redskins were only seven points behind. If they could score another touchdown, the teams would be tied.

But the Dolphins' luck held out. They won, 14–7. Garo's pass had not cost them the championship. And he hoped it would soon be forgotten.

To Garo's surprise, his funny pass gave him new fame. Someone even wrote a song about his pass. Garo sang the song on a record. And many fans bought it to hear Garo sing. Garo also spoke about his pass at sports dinners. He laughed at himself. And football fans all over laughed with him.

Hard to Go in the Snow

December 19, 1948. The
Philadelphia Eagles were planning
to play the Chicago Cardinals in
Philadelphia. The game would decide
the National Football League
championship.

The day turned out to be the worst
one of the year. The temperature was
below freezing. And snow had been
falling all morning. The weatherman
said there would be at least two feet of
it before the storm ended.

Weather almost never stops a
football game. But this was a real
blizzard. The falling snow had
completely covered the football field.

Should the game be played on another day? Bert Bell, who was commissioner of the league, had to make the decision. The Eagle coach wanted to call off the game. The Cardinal coach wanted to play. Commissioner Bell decided to let the game go on.

The snow did not keep the Eagle fans away. Nearly 29,000 of them came to the stadium. They all wanted to see the NFL championship game.

Before the opening kickoff, the players helped lift the covering (a tarpaulin) from the field. It had so much snow on it that the grounds crew needed help. As soon as the tarpaulin was taken away, the snow quickly covered the field.

Eagles and Cardinals lift the tarpaulin.

Then the lights went on. They brightened the field a little. But the players still had a hard time seeing anything through the falling snow.

The opening kickoff went to the Cardinals. They tried running the ball up the field. But the ground was too slippery. The day was going to be a long one for both teams.

Running was almost impossible. And the ball was too cold and slippery for much passing or catching. Also, the players could not see far enough to throw very long passes. But both teams played as hard as they could. Even so, at the half the score was 0–0.

Late in the third quarter, the Eagles jumped on a Cardinal fumble. They had the ball on the Cardinal 17-yard line. Perhaps they could score.

On their first play, the Eagles gained

five yards. Then the third quarter
ended.

The teams moved to the other end
of the field. As they moved, they made
fresh footprints in the heavy snow.

In two more plays, the Eagles
pushed to the Cardinals' 5-yard line.
Then on the next play, Philadelphia's
Steve Van Buren carried the ball over
the goal. He made a touchdown. One
of the teams had scored at last!

The one and only touchdown.

The Eagles cleared some ground for the extra point try. The kick was good. The Eagles were ahead, 7–0.

The Cardinals tried hard for the rest of the quarter. But they could not score. The cold and the snow were too much for them. When the game ended, the score was still Eagles 7, Cardinals 0.

Five inches of snow had fallen during the game. It was amazing that anyone had scored at all in such a terrible blizzard.

The Eagles after the game.

Plum to Plum

Who kicked the longest field goal? Who threw the longest complete pass? The answers to these questions and many others are in the football record book.

Each year some records are broken. But here is the story of one that may never be broken.

October 18, 1959. The Cleveland Browns were playing the Chicago Cardinals. Cleveland's quarterback that day was Milt Plum.

The game was going well for the Browns. Toward the end of the second half they were leading, 17–0.

But people in the stands were getting restless. They wanted action.

Milt Plum

And neither team was moving the ball.

Then the Browns got the ball again. They moved it 5 yards in two plays. They needed 5 more yards on the next play.

Cleveland fans began to yell for a

first-down play. Milt Plum had already thrown one touchdown pass. They hoped he would throw another.

The Cleveland center snapped the ball into Plum's hands. Plum ran back, getting set to pass. The Cardinals rushed after him.

Plum looked down the field. He finally found a free man on the left sideline. Plum threw the football to him.

But the man did not catch it. Instead, a Cardinal lineman swung at the ball—and hit it. The football flew back at Plum. The surprised quarterback caught his own pass.

Right away Plum started racing down the field. He ran 20 yards before he was tackled.

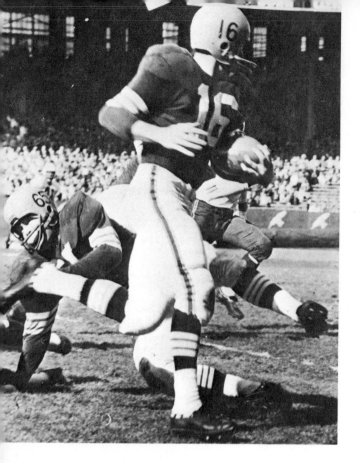

Cleveland had its first down. Milt Plum had a new football record. He had caught his own pass and gained 20 yards.

When the game ended, the Browns were on top, 17–7. The game had been like any other—except for one amazing play. Milt Plum's pass to Milt Plum is still in the record book. And it may be there forever.

Off the Bench

September 15, 1935. The Green Bay Packers were playing the Chicago Bears in Chicago. The game was the second of the year for the Packers. But it was the first for rookie Don Hutson.

Hutson had been a great star in college. But this year was his first in pro football. He had never played in a professional game before. He had watched the Packers' first game from the bench. No one knew how the young end would do against the Bears.

The Packers won the coin toss. They quickly lined up and waited for the Bears' kickoff. The Bears' kick sailed into the end zone.

Don Hutson

The Packers' fullback took the ball and started up the field. He reached the 17-yard line. Then the Bears hit him hard and stopped him. The Chicago fans roared. Already they were sure that their team was going to beat the Packers.

A few seconds later the Packers lined up. Don Hutson got set for his first play in pro football.

The ball came back to Arnie Herber, the Packers' star backfield man. He backed up and looked down the field. The Bears were rushing at him.

Herber looked again. He was hoping to get off a surprise pass. Then he spotted young Don Hutson. He pulled his arm back and let the ball fly. He threw a long pass. It surprised the Bears. They were not ready for such a long pass.

The ball carried for 50 yards. Herber had thrown a perfect pass. And when the ball came down, young Don Hutson made a perfect catch.

The Packers' new end started racing for the goal line. The surprised Bears started racing after him. But they could not catch young Don Hutson. Seconds later he raced across the goal for a Packer touchdown.

Don Hutson had scored a touchdown on his first play in professional football! The Packers kicked for the extra point, and that was the last scoring in the game. The Packers won, 7–0.

When the teams ran off the field, the fans stood and cheered Don Hutson. His catch—on his first play in professional football—had won the game.

For Don Hutson, it was a great day. It was the first of many great days. Soon he became one of the big stars of pro football.

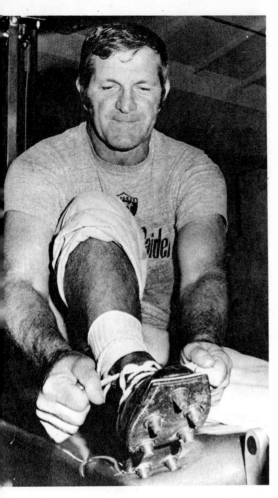

The Old Man

In 1970 George Blanda was playing for the Oakland Raiders. He was 43 years old—the oldest man ever to play professional football. And he had been playing it for 21 years.

Pro football is a hard game. Players don't often play past the age of 35. Younger and stronger men take their places. But the amazing George Blanda surprised football fans and football players. The older he got, the better he seemed to play. At 43 he could kick field goals and play quarterback as well as anyone in professional football.

In 1970 Blanda had an amazing playing streak—for a man of any age. In two straight games he came off the bench to lead the Raiders to a win and a tie.

Then on November 8 the Raiders went to Cleveland to play the Browns. At the end of the first quarter the Raiders were leading, 3–0. But the Browns fought back. In the fourth quarter, the score was Browns 17, Raiders 13. The Raiders were counting on quarterback Daryle Lamonica to save the game.

But then a hard tackle hurt Lamonica. He was out of the game. The Oakland coach turned to Blanda and said, "Get in there, George." Could Blanda lead the Raiders to another win?

He started badly. The Browns caught his first pass. Then they scored a field goal. Now the Raiders were behind, 20–13.

The next kickoff put the Raiders on their own 31-yard line. With just four minutes left in the game, Blanda got ready to pass. He knew that this was the last chance for his team.

Blanda threw three more passes. He moved the Raiders 44 yards down the field. But on the next play, the Browns threw Blanda down before he could pass. Time was running out for the Old Man and the Raiders.

Blanda stayed calm. His next pass got the team a first down. He followed

with a touchdown pass. The kick for the extra point was good. The score was 20–20 with little more than a minute left to play.

The Browns were trying hard. But the Raiders grabbed one of their passes.

The Oakland team took over near midfield. With 34 seconds left in the game, the Old Man came out for one last try.

Blanda threw two passes. But both of them missed. Only three seconds were left. Blanda got into place for a kick. He was going to try for a field goal. In order to score, he would have to kick the ball 52 yards.

The ball was set in place. Blanda kicked. The ball flew into the air. The kick was good! The Raiders won, 23–20. For the third time Blanda had saved the day for the Raiders.

The Old Man's passing and kicking amazed football fans all over the country. But he had more surprises for them.

Blanda kicks a field goal.

In the next two Raider games, Blanda again came off the bench to lead Oakland to wins.

In all, Blanda came in and saved five games in a row. For a professional football player he was an old man. But his amazing playing proved that he did not think so.

Racing Against the Clock

November 5, 1967—Baltimore. The Colts were playing the Green Bay Packers.

The Baltimore fans were not feeling happy that day. Over and over again, the Packers stopped the Colts. With a little more than two minutes left in the game, the Packers were leading, 10–0. The Colt fans had little hope that their team could catch up.

The Colts play the Packers.

But then Johnny Unitas, the Colts' star quarterback, began to move his team up the field. In play after play he gained yards for the Colts. He ended with a 10-yard touchdown pass. It lifted the fans out of their seats. Their team still had a chance either to win or to tie the game. But the Colts had to race against the clock. They had little more than two minutes to catch up to the Packers.

Seconds later the Baltimore fans stopped cheering. The kick for the extra point was not good. Time was running out. The Colts were losing, 10–6. If the extra point had been good, they might have been able to tie the game with a field goal. Now they needed a touchdown, or they would lose. And the kickoff was going to the Packers.

With two minutes left to play, the teams lined up for the kickoff. Baltimore kicked the ball. A Packer touched the ball. But he could not hold onto it. A Colt player broke through and jumped on it.

Now the Colts had the ball on the Packer 34-yard line. The clock showed that there was a little more than 90 seconds left in the game. That was enough time for the Colts to score. But the Packers were not going to let the game get away from them—if they could help it.

On three quick plays the Colts gained only 4 yards. It was fourth down and 6 yards to go for the Colts.

Johnny Unitas

If they could not gain 6 yards on this play, they would lose the ball.

The ball was snapped to Johnny Unitas. He ran back, getting ready to pass. But he could not find a man in the clear. And the Packers were moving in on him.

Then Unitas made a surprise move.

He ran with the ball! The Packers
threw him down. But they were too
late. Unitas had gained 7 yards,
enough for a first down. With a little
more than a minute left, the Colts still
had a chance.

On the next play, Johnny Unitas
again ran back to pass. This time he
found a man in the clear and threw to
him. The man caught the ball. He ran
all the way to the goal.

Unitas (19) throws the ball.

The Colts had scored a touchdown.
The kick for the extra point was good,
too. The Baltimore crowd stood and
cheered. Now the Colts were ahead,
13–10.

The Packers tried to fight back. But
time ran out. The Colts won the game.
The fans yelled and clapped for
Johnny Unitas. In little more than two
minutes, his great running and passing
had changed the game. He had won
the race against the clock.

An Amazing Tackle

January 1, 1954. The game was the Cotton Bowl Championship in Dallas, Texas. The two great college teams playing in it were Alabama and Rice.

Alabama's hopes were not high. Several players had been hurt. And they were not going to be able to play. Alabama would have to do some great playing to beat Rice.

But Alabama became more hopeful in the first quarter. Their star fullback, Tommy Lewis, fought his way across the goal line. His touchdown gave Alabama a 6–0 lead at the end of the first quarter.

Rice fans sat back and waited. They were sure Rice's halfback, Dicky Moegle (MAY-gull), would score in the second quarter. And they were right.

On the very first play of the second quarter, Moegle got the ball. He raced around the Alabama players and ran 79 yards for a touchdown. With a good kick for the extra point, Rice took a 7–6 lead.

The Alabama players quickly fought back. They moved the ball to the Rice 5-yard line. They were close to a touchdown. Alabama fans stood up and cheered. But on the next play they groaned. Alabama fumbled. With only a few minutes left in the half, the ball went over to Rice.

The Rice players lined up on their

5-yard line. Alabama's line faced them. From his bench on the sidelines, Alabama fullback Tommy Lewis watched closely. He hoped his team would hold the line. He did not want Rice to score again.

The ball went to Dicky Moegle. Following some good blockers, he rushed around the right end. Then he started up the right sideline. The Rice fans roared.

Moegle picked up speed as he moved up the field. He crossed his 45-yard line. No Alabama player could stop him now.

At midfield, the players on the Alabama bench watched Moegle speed past. Tommy Lewis was one of them. Suddenly Lewis jumped off the bench.

Follow the arrow: Tommy Lewis comes off the bench.

He tackles Dicky Moegle.

He leaves the field.

He rushed onto the field and tackled Moegle! Then he rushed back to the bench.

The fans could not believe their eyes. And Dicky Moegle could not believe what had happened to him. He was down on the Alabama 38-yard line. He had been tackled by a man who was not even in the game.

Lewis had broken a rule. The referee picked up the ball and carried it over the goal line. He was giving Moegle a touchdown. The play went into the records as a 95-yard run for Rice.

On the bench Lewis hid his face in his hands. He kept telling himself, "I didn't do it. I didn't do it."

Later Moegle scored another touchdown. Rice won by a final score of 28–6.

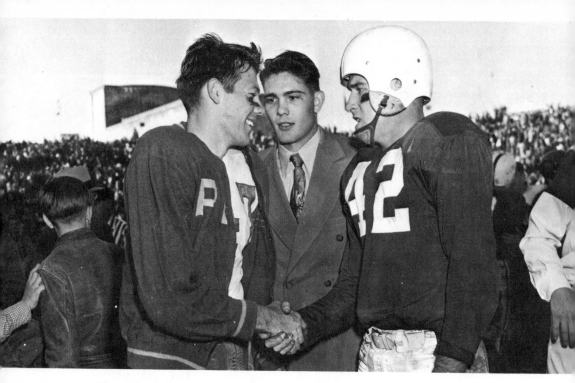

Tommy Lewis apologizes to Dicky Moegle.

For his part in the game, Moegle got the Most Valuable Player award. But Lewis' amazing tackle was the event the fans would never forget. Lewis would never forget it either. His pride in Alabama had made him jump off the bench to help his team win the game.

Running Wild

December 12, 1965, was a cold day in Chicago. But 46,000 fans came out to see the Bears play the San Francisco Forty-Niners. The Chicago fans were hoping that Gale Sayers, the Bears' new star back, would give them a game to remember.

Gale Sayers was playing his very first year in professional football. After only 12 games he had become a star. He was a fast runner and was great at catching passes. Already he had scored 15 touchdowns.

In the first quarter, Gale Sayers showed the fans what they wanted to see. He caught a short pass and ran 80 yards for a touchdown.

In the second quarter, Sayers really made his fans happy. First he scored a touchdown on a 21-yard run. Then he made another touchdown on a 7-yard run. At halftime, the score was Bears 27, Forty-Niners 13. Gale Sayers had scored 18 of the 27 points with his three touchdowns.

Gale Sayers scores a touchdown.

When the teams came on the field for the third quarter, the fans cheered for Gale Sayers. He had been running wild. They hoped he would keep going.

And he did! On one play Sayers raced through the line and kept going for 50 yards. He made another touchdown. Before the third quarter ended, he scored again. The Bears were leading, 40–13. And 30 points came from Gale Sayers' five touchdowns.

Early in the fourth quarter, the Forty-Niners and the Bears each made a touchdown. The score was Bears 47, San Francisco 20. The Forty-Niners were not going to catch up to the Bears. Even so, the fans wanted more action from Gale Sayers.

Sayers needed one more touchdown to tie a record. In 1929 Ernie Nevers had scored six touchdowns in one game. In 1951 "Dub" Jones had done the same thing. They shared the record for the most touchdowns scored by one man in a single game. Both men had set their records while playing against the Chicago Bears. Now the Chicago fans wanted Sayers to tie that record.

Minutes later, Gale Sayers caught a kick on his own 15-yard line. He started up the field. He picked up speed as he ran. The Forty-Niners tried hard to stop him. But Gale Sayers was not going to let anybody stop him. He raced 85 yards for a touchdown. The record was tied! He had scored his sixth touchdown of the game!

A happy Gale Sayers.

When Gale Sayers ran off the field, the fans came out of their seats cheering. His running was the greatest they had ever seen. And it was only his first year in professional football.

At the end of the game, the score was Bears 61, Forty-Niners 20. Gale Sayers had scored 36 of the Bears' 61 points. He had made six touchdowns, and had tied a record. December 12, 1965, was a great day for Gale Sayers.